Unbreakable Spirit

Unbreakable Spirit

Gideon Rayburn

Contents

1   Chapter 1: Introduction to Resilience   **1**

2   Chapter 2: The Importance of Resilience in Modern   **5**

3   Chapter 3: Psychological Foundations of Resilience   **9**

4   Chapter 4: Developing Resilience Skills   **13**

5   Chapter 5: Cultural and Societal Influences on Res   **17**

6   Chapter 6: Resilience in Different Life Stages   **21**

7   Chapter 7: Physical Health and Resilience   **25**

8   Chapter 8: Resilience in the Face of Specific Chal   **29**

9   Chapter 9: The Role of Social Support in Building   **33**

10   Chapter 10: Resilience and Innovation   **37**

11   Chapter 11: Resilience in Leadership   **41**

12   Chapter 12: Measuring and Assessing Resilience   **45**

13   Chapter 13: Ethical Considerations in Resilience R   **49**

14   Chapter 14: The Future of Resilience Research   **53**

15   Chapter 15: Conclusion and Practical Applications   **57**

{ 1 }

Chapter 1: Introduction to Resilience

What is Resilience?

The American Psychological Association (APA) defines resilience as "The process of adapting well in the face of adversity, trauma, tragedy, threats, or significant sources of stress - such as family and relationship problems, serious health problems, and workplace and financial stressors... It means 'bouncing back' from difficult experiences."

However, resilience is more than just maintaining a façade of happiness or being unaffected during tumultuous times. It involves actively recovering from challenges, setbacks, or traumas, whether minor or significant, with a sense of strength and wholeheartedness. Resilience is not about the absence of emotions; it's about managing them effectively. It involves maintaining control, reducing the influence of negative emotions, and accurately interpreting their relevance.

People who are resilient do not ignore pain and negativity; they acknowledge and address it, often with humor, attention, or a lesson learned. They manage to keep a constructive perspective despite the difficulties they face. Resilience is not merely enduring hardship but mastering it by believing in a positive outcome. It is not a fixed trait but a dynamic process that can be developed over time. By acting intentionally in ways that optimize energy, resist distraction, and minimize damage, we can cultivate resilience.

The Nature of Resilience

Resilience allows individuals to let each lesson inform them without letting it define them. It helps them overcome obstacles, knowing that these bumps in the road are opportunities for growth both personally and professionally. Resilient people face challenges head-on, drawing on their strengths and the support of others, such as family, friends, and mentors. These supports provide a sense of meaning and purpose, making life's journey more significant.

Resilience is an empowering quality essential for success in personal and professional life. In a demanding world, resilience can make the difference between merely meeting expectations and exceeding them. Resilient individuals accept adversity, showing courage, resourcefulness, and patience. They believe in their ability to rebuild their lives despite disappointments and frustrations. They know that within them lies the key to a successful recovery.

Defining Resilience

It's crucial to differentiate resilience from mere happiness or zest. While zest involves a joyful enjoyment of life's moments, resilience often arises from challenging or dismal periods. Medal of Honor winner and former presidential candidate General George S. Patton aptly said, "Courage is fear holding on a minute longer." He also noted, "There is but one test of character, the ability to meet and master whatever betide us." Thus, resilience is fundamentally different from high spirits, happiness, or even hope.

Resilience enables individuals to manage suffering and hardship, allowing them to grow through these experiences. At its most mature expression, resilience allows people to learn from adversity and transform suffering into something positive. This growth often leads to increased empathy and a deeper sense of purpose. In essence, resilience is not just about surviving life's challenges but thriving despite them.

Historical Perspectives on Resilience

Historical perspectives on resilience suggest that suffering and distress offer unique paths to wisdom and enlightenment. Different views of resilience place it within a broader context of human spirituality, health, sustenance, and well-being. According to the 3D School of Resilience, resilience is "a universal capacity that allows a person, group, or community to prevent, minimize, overcome adverse effects of adversity, cope with misfortune, return to good standing, and do so in ways that both protect and promote his and her own well-being and development." This definition emphasizes the importance of resilience on personal, familial, social, and spiritual levels.

The concept of resilience has roots in ancient philosophy, often attributed to Aristotle. The term describes a quality that enables individuals to recover from misfortune and lead a life of health, good spirits, and the pursuit of happiness. Adversity provides insights into the human experience, and overcoming tough times with grace and perseverance showcases our humanity. From ancient to modern times, resilience has been viewed as a valuable quality that allows individuals to grow and thrive despite challenges.

{ 2 }

Chapter 2: The Importance of Resilience in Modern

The Changing Landscape of Resilience

As our support networks evolve and traditional coping mechanisms fade, the behaviors once encouraged by these signs are transforming, often to our detriment. Arguments that greater resilience might reinforce these mechanisms can seem contrafactual. Imagine the deeply stressed business traveler navigating the chaos of a bustling airport, bombarded by noise, light, and relentless advertising. It's hard to see how this environment could enhance her humanity. The pervasive push from commercial enterprises to deliver constant self-affirmation through a barrage of advertising often distorts our understanding of genuine progress and value.

In the Information Age, we find ourselves less resilient when facing failure or disappointment. With tools becoming easier to use and horizons broadening, both effort and failure are stretched beyond reasonable limits. We no longer need to remember key information like phone numbers and birthdays. Why develop these skills if they seem unnecessary? As information technology amplifies success, it also highlights even minor failures, emphasizing human limitations. This is especially true in cultures that emphasize individual choice, mobility, and the pursuit of knowledge. In such an environment, even subtle imperfections can stand out.

Resilience in the Workplace

Rapid changes in policies, work performance expectations, or the physical workspace can lead to pressure and instability. For instance, a business that maintains service levels despite declining profits might appear resilient. However, a business that quickly pivots and introduces new services in response to hardship demonstrates true resilience and long-term sustainability. This resilience is often supported by the collective culture and the individual resilience of employees, allowing the company to seize new opportunities amid business volatility.

In the workplace, flexibility and adaptability are crucial. As work changes and control diminishes, resilience becomes a top skill. Successful employers in the coming decades will likely be those with resilient workforces. Resilience in the workplace is about overcoming change and challenges and bouncing back to greatness. Economic downturns, management changes, and restructuring are just a few hurdles. Employees are expected to take on extra work and adjust to new workflows, demonstrating resilience.

Resilience in Education

Resilience can be significantly developed in educational settings. Studies on teacher training interventions and social-emotional learning programs show that teachers can enhance children's social-emotional skills and resilience. Teaching resilience involves several steps: evaluating learning experiences, engaging students at multiple levels, developing stress reduction and emotional balance systems, embedding contemplative practices in the classroom, utilizing reflection, and explicitly teaching resilience skills.

The rapid pace of change in the world presents challenges. Shifts in family structures, dual-income households, and increased divorce rates contribute to the complexity of issues schools face. Schools struggle with academic accountability and improvement plans while managing marketing, mentoring, and data responsibilities. Resilience, therefore, becomes a crucial skill.

Resilience plays a critical role in individual well-being and success. Children who can cope with adversity are more likely to succeed in school and work. They are less likely to develop psychological, health, social, and behavioral issues when they can manage life's challenges. Today's teachers are responsible for teaching basic knowledge, 21st-century skills, character, values, and now, resilience.

Chapter 3: Psychological Foundations of Resilience

Positive Reinterpretation and Growth

Positive reinterpretation and growth have been observed even in people facing seemingly unbearable circumstances, such as life-threatening illnesses. While no studies have yet fully explored the predictors of adversity-related growth among dying individuals, existing research shows growth is associated with various psychological variables, including struggle, distress, positive mental health attributes, and the harsh realities of appearance-related behavior. Spiritual growth often correlates with dimensions of vulnerability, distress, and personal focus. As researchers delve deeper into understanding the discrepancy between physical and psychological interpretations of pathology among terminally ill patients, this area of study is poised to expand significantly.

Uncovering the psychological clues to resilience is akin to solving a profound mystery. Adversity endured, learning transformed into growth, and comfort achieved is perhaps the most common human narrative. What elevates resilience to the realm of "art" is the style with which individuals navigate this process—not necessarily beauty, but the ability to create order out of chaos. Resilience involves dealing with life's knocks and getting back on our feet. Emotion regulation techniques are crucial for reframing adversity and thriving afterward. Mindfulness, in particular, is an effective skill in this context, while emotion suppression and rumination can be harmful.

Theories of Resilience

There is notable tension between two primary perspectives on resilience. The first perspective focuses on the individual, often neglecting the roles played by family, community, and society. This view underestimates the importance of context, including institutional support, structural resources, and broader social inequalities. The second perspective, on the other hand, conceptualizes inequity and suffering as intertwined, suggesting that certain groups may never escape failure or find resilience. Both approaches fail to incorporate a dystopian stance, as suggested by scholars like Diesendruck and Yofee, who emphasize the need to continually struggle to operate effectively under adverse conditions.

Two main theoretical perspectives help us understand how resilience emerges. The first perspective, rooted in the inherent resources and strength of the individual, emphasizes cultural strength and the capacity to develop resilience, as highlighted by transcultural psychologist Yehuda Bauer. This view often centers on individual development at the expense of understanding the complex ecosystemic contexts in which people live. The second perspective, Critical Resilience, focuses on socio-political factors. It suggests that resilience becomes salient in the context of power relations within society. Issues of social justice, marginalization, and disadvantage are crucial for understanding the strength and adaptability of marginalized groups and those who advocate against institutionalized inequality.

Resilience and Mental Health

Research by Scott and colleagues highlights that an individual's ability to cope with everyday demands, work productively, and contribute to society is closely linked to resilience. Resilience is also a key component of positive psychology, determining one's mental health trajectory and recovery from traumatic experiences. Individuals with low resilience may struggle or take longer to recover from conditions, even when participating in effective interventions. Thus, resilience plays a central role in the prevention, recovery, and treatment of mental health issues. It helps reduce long-term mental health problems following adversities and supports mental well-being despite exposure to challenges.

Mental health is a significant aspect of recovery from adversity. Studies have shown a relationship between post-traumatic growth and resilience. Post-traumatic growth refers to positive changes experienced due to struggling with highly challenging life crises. It is inversely related to negative mental health effects following serious traumas. Post-traumatic growth outcomes include greater appreciation for life and changed life priorities. Research suggests that such positive outcomes can amplify the transmission of resilience and may offer mechanisms for understanding the developmental course of mental health issues resulting from trauma.

Chapter 4: Developing Resilience Skills

Active Strategies for Influencing Tough Situations
Identifying meaningful active strategies can help you manage tough personal situations. Having a plan and being willing to implement it can reduce feelings of powerlessness and stress during difficult times. Here are a few examples:

- **Daily Walks:** Instead of letting your dog out in the yard, take him for daily walks. This not only provides companionship but also encourages physical activity, which can improve your mood and overall well-being.
- **Outdoor Seating:** If your home or school is busy and overwhelming, adding outdoor seating can offer a quiet retreat. A peaceful outdoor space can serve as a sanctuary for relaxation and reflection.
- **Main Living Area Care:** For those dealing with ill health, moving daily essential care functions to main living areas can make caretaking activities feel less isolated and dehumanizing. By integrating these activities into common spaces, caretakers and patients can feel more connected and involved in daily life.

These strategies help change situations, making them more manageable and less stressful.

Skills for Building Resilience

Implementing resilience-building skills can protect against worry and feelings of helplessness. Life's challenges can lead to burnout or a desire to withdraw from social interactions. The following six resilience skills can help you perform at your best while maintaining balance and vitality:

1. **Healthy Thinking Styles:** Cultivating healthy thinking styles is foundational. Just as roots anchor a tree, positive thinking anchors resilience. Mental coping strategies, like leaves and branches, make us flexible and capable of withstanding life's blows.

2. **Positive Reappraisal:** This involves viewing a difficult situation in a more positive light, identifying the silver linings in life's challenges. This technique helps maintain a positive outlook amid adversity.

3. **Emotional Acceptance:** Acknowledging and accepting your emotions, rather than suppressing them, fosters resilience. Understanding and processing emotions lead to healthier outcomes.

4. **Cognitive Reappraisal:** Thinking about stressful situations as challenges rather than threats can change your perspective and enhance resilience.

5. **Strength Use:** Leveraging your strengths and abilities can help you navigate tough times more effectively. Recognizing and utilizing your strengths builds confidence and resilience.

6. **Humor and Social Support:** Humor and social support are powerful resilience tools. Laughter and connections with

others provide emotional relief and practical support during challenging times.

Cognitive Strategies for Building Resilience

Healthy thinking styles and mental coping strategies are essential for flexibility and resilience. Here are ten psychological techniques that can make stressful events less problematic:

1. **Optimism:** Cultivate a positive outlook on life. Optimism helps you see challenges as opportunities for growth.
2. **Self-Compassion:** Treat yourself with kindness and understanding, especially during difficult times.
3. **Problem-Solving:** Develop effective problem-solving skills to tackle challenges head-on.
4. **Goal Setting:** Set realistic and achievable goals. Working towards these goals provides a sense of purpose and direction.
5. **Mindfulness:** Practice mindfulness to stay present and focused. Mindfulness helps you manage stress and maintain emotional balance.
6. **Gratitude:** Foster a sense of gratitude for what you have. Gratitude can shift your focus from what's going wrong to what's going well.
7. **Resilience Visualization:** Visualize yourself successfully overcoming challenges. This mental rehearsal can enhance confidence and resilience.
8. **Flexibility:** Be open to change and adapt to new circumstances. Flexibility allows you to adjust your plans as needed.
9. **Emotional Regulation:** Develop techniques to manage and regulate your emotions effectively.

10. **Support Networks:** Build and maintain strong support networks. Friends, family, and colleagues can provide invaluable support during tough times.

Emotional Regulation Techniques

Neuroscientific research suggests that variance in the control-related dopamine system may explain why some individuals are more resilient than others. The left lateral prefrontal cortex plays a crucial role in regulating emotions, preparing individuals to respond better to unruly emotions. Meditation, biofeedback, and psychotherapeutic treatments can enhance the brain's capacity for emotional regulation.

Several emotional regulation techniques can cultivate resilience:

- **Positive Reappraisal:** This technique involves reinterpreting negative events in a more positive light, helping you stay afloat in a sea of distress.
- **Emotional Acceptance:** Accepting your emotions rather than suppressing them leads to healthier outcomes.
- **Cognitive Reappraisal:** Viewing stressful situations as challenges instead of threats can improve your resilience.
- **Humor:** Finding humor in difficult situations can provide emotional relief and a different perspective.
- **Emotional Intelligence:** Developing emotional intelligence helps you understand and manage your emotions effectively.
- **Social Support:** Building strong social networks provides practical and emotional support during challenging times.

Chapter 5: Cultural and Societal Influences on Res

Social, Economic, and Historical Conditions

The art of resilience is not solely determined by individual factors like temperament, powers of persuasion, or sense of purpose. Underlying the skills and attitudes that contribute to resilience are social, economic, and historical conditions. For instance, children growing up in isolated, impoverished, crime-ridden neighborhoods are less likely to develop resilience. The more adverse conditions they experience, the higher their levels of personal risk. Poverty, whether in developing or developed countries, is one of the greatest risk factors, linked to poor parenting skills, toxic environmental conditions, social exclusion, stress and depression, and reduced access to quality education, healthcare, and other services.

Community is also a crucial source of resilience. Numerous studies have shown that social support can buffer individuals from the impact of adversity. People better integrated into their families, peer groups, communities, and cultures are more capable of withstanding stress and tend to be healthier. For example, Yugoslavian prisoners of war who remained resilient and emerged without lasting psychological scars were those who felt most connected to their colleagues. Beyond small groups, cultural entities like religious organizations and charitable societies can also foster resilience. Community spirit and religious faith can dramatically enhance well-being by providing meaning and hope during difficult times, helping individuals reinterpret their experiences positively.

Cross-Cultural Perspectives on Resilience

In a recent review, researcher Windle noted the significant increase in the quantity and quality of resilience research over the past few decades. Despite various approaches to conceptualizing and measuring resilience, a common defining feature is that it is a dynamic phenomenon. Resilience is evident in the maintenance or recovery of valuable outcomes that might have been lost. Most comprehensive models of resilience acknowledge the existence of multiple potential paths to resilience. One of the key principles, known as the differential activation hypothesis (DAH), suggests that the effectiveness of resilience strategies depends on a person's current and past experiences.

Recent interest in resilience stems from its potential to enhance mental and physical health despite adversity. Efforts to understand and enhance resilience can be particularly beneficial to individuals facing challenges. There is also interest in exploring whether methods to build resilience should be conceptualized and implemented differently across cultural contexts. This chapter reviews extensive research on resilience and examines distinctions between stability at the individual and broader cultural levels.

Community Resilience

Several definitions of resilience in the context of disaster research emphasize the ability to prepare for, absorb, recover from, or adapt to adverse events. Adversity affects both individuals and communities, requiring adaptation and intentional development to cope with potential suffering. Resilience research often focuses on the energy or resources needed to respond effectively to disasters.

The concept of resilience was first introduced by Canadian ecologists Crawford S. Holling and Lance H. Gunderson, who studied ecosystem recovery capacities. This concept has since been applied to human communities, emphasizing the importance of protection and destruction processes in disaster management. Resilience assessment guides the development and application of approaches to leverage opportunities and identify potential responses to disaster risks. It also considers the future condition of social-ecological systems, ensuring that communities can sustain and enhance their adaptive capacities.

In essence, resilience within communities involves the capacity to operate, be flexible, learn, and maintain necessary functions in the face of adversity. By understanding and applying resilience concepts, communities can better prepare for and respond to challenges, shaping future risks and improving overall well-being.

Chapter 6: Resilience in Different Life Stages

Societal Contributions to Resilience

Populations who withstand disasters exhibit several resilience-related characteristics: engaging in preparation, maintaining themselves and their societies, and receiving support from their communities. Clear communication, monitoring, and protection by citizens, organizations, and governmental agencies play vital roles. Awareness and proactive actions contribute to prevention, reduction, and education. The responses before, during, and after adversities shape and define populations that bounce back.

Reducing societal divisiveness and discrimination is crucial in combating adversity. Children, in particular, suffer from a lack of care and community support. Limited resources and parental stress can lead to health problems such as early heart disease, obesity, tooth decay, and behavioral issues. When teachers integrate social support into the classroom, children learn better, work harder, and exhibit academic, behavioral, and emotional resilience.

A supportive environment fosters increased social responsibility within a community. This reciprocity can occur within families, between friends, in neighborhoods, and religious communities. Faith and personal philosophies provide organizational and communal resources that buffer adversity, teaching principles and techniques for thriving amid turmoil and discouraging antisocial behavior. Religious leaders and schoolteachers, through their roles as authority figures, can teach resilience-oriented curricula and non-curricula, guiding their communities through challenging times.

Life Stages and Resilience

Resilience is not only a quality but a process influenced by different life stages. How we handle adversities as children, teenagers, and adults is affected by our health, personalities, and social niches. We are fundamentally social creatures, and our intimate relationships influence our immune, endocrine, and nervous systems, either positively or negatively. Cultivating socially supportive relationships and services reduces early causes of disease and suffering across cultures.

Resilience in Childhood

Children with secure attachments can explore the world, knowing their parents are available for support. Resilient children can organize memories for positive developmental learning and recover from failures. Children who survive a primary caregiver's depression often experience communication about the condition and family mental health problems, finding ways to protect themselves from parental sadness and suffering.

Throughout each developmental stage, children face various situations. With a strong mental foundation, they consider these manageable. Adults play a crucial role in helping children reflect on their victories, promoting self-awareness that aids in facing future problems. The family's health, resources, and coping skills are the first influences on a child's resilience. Early relationships with parents, especially the mother, are critical. Emotionally available or sensitive mothers foster secure attachments, contributing to a child's well-being and exploratory behavior. Morning interactions, where predictable patterns are established, likely create healthy resilience functioning in a child's development. Parental coping and general mental and physical health are also vital.

Resilience in Older Adults

Older adults who find meaning in life despite hardship remain open to new experiences and flexible in their approaches. Successful aging involves adaptation, allowing older adults to invest resources in what they care about. Qualities like connectedness, tolerance, and responsibility are often present. Spiritual meaning in life, found in valued relationships, good health, and social activity, reduces loneliness and enhances well-being. Religious involvement, emphasizing community, supports positive aging and resilience by fostering connections with others and the outside world. Resilience in aging does not eliminate stress and losses but facilitates a final healing, providing meaning and a sense of radiance.

While growing older does not automatically bestow wisdom or coping ability, older adults are not deprived of resilience by metabolism alone. Resilience in older adults is often shaped by various life experiences, including positive early relationships, personal strength-building experiences, successful encounters with life's challenges, and a deep appreciation for one's journey. These experiences support the development of resilience-associated qualities like secure attachment, autonomy, self-efficacy, responsibility, and integrity. They also enhance empathy, love, realistic self-appraisals, and a commitment to living fully. Older adults who have faced and overcome challenges tend to possess traits like energy, compassion, humor, and psychological flexibility, which make life enjoyable and suggest resilience has been achieved.

Chapter 7: Physical Health and Resilience

The Role of Physical Activity in Resilience
Evidence suggests that even light exercise, such as a leisurely walk, can reduce depression, a common side effect of adversity. The advantages of exercise are multifaceted, impacting both physical and emotional well-being.

- **Physical Fitness**: Enhances muscular and cardiovascular health, contributing to overall brain health and better coping mechanisms for adverse stimuli.
- **Emotional Resilience**: Regular exercise reduces anxiety and alleviates psychological symptoms like fatigue, emotional stress, muscle tension, depression, anger, and disturbed sleep. It fosters a sense of relief from these burdens.

Engaging in Physical Activity

Regular exercise that leads to muscle contraction helps release tension, reduce chemical by-products in muscles, and promote muscle recovery. It also trains the cardiovascular system and increases blood flow, enhancing brain function and promoting a fresher, more resilient state of mind. Aim for at least thirty minutes of moderate-intensity exercise with muscle tension most days of the week. Activities like brisk walking, running, cycling, and swimming are effective options.

The Mind-Body Connection

A story shared by Rabbi Abraham Twerski in his book "The Art of Serenity" illustrates the profound mind-body connection. A man suffering from high blood pressure and the need to lose weight took a month in a government weight loss program. Through daily exercise and time spent alone in nature, he transformed his health and outlook on life. This anecdote underscores the age-old concept of "mens sana in corpore sano" - a sound mind in a sound body. Advocates of the mind-body connection emphasize its timeless relevance in fostering resilience.

Nutrition and Resilience

Proper nutrition is crucial for promoting resilience as it provides the basic building blocks for cellular function and structure, influences cognitive function, affects mood, and interacts significantly with the stress response.

- **Cognitive Development**: A poor-quality diet can hinder brain growth and learning ability during development and lead to cognitive decline in old age. Good dietary habits, initiated in childhood, help the brain reach its potential and prevent mental decline.
- **Mental Performance**: Undernutrition impacts all aspects of the body, including tissue growth and repair, organ function, and mental performance. Combined with chronic illness and stress, undernutrition can result in the failure of the body to grow and develop properly.

The Importance of Nutrition

Research supports the idea that proper nutrition can enhance resilience to adversity. Diets rich in essential nutrients help the brain function optimally, influence mood positively, and provide the energy needed to cope with stress. While there's no way to "eat your way to a superbrain," good dietary habits significantly contribute to maintaining mental and physical health, especially during challenging times.

Chapter 8: Resilience in the Face of Specific Chal

Drawing Inspiration from Role Models
Finding and learning from the stories of people who inspire you can be incredibly powerful. For instance, my parents are my role models. I draw strength from my faith and feel a responsibility to serve my community. The wisdom of my culture, rooted in ages of wars and colonization, teaches me resourcefulness and resilience. This legacy inspires me to stand firm and move forward with joy. Through generations, we have faced loss, tragedy, and the unexpected. Our laughter, creativity, and perseverance have sustained us and continue to do so. In my people's history, we have survived bitter times, calling for courage, endurance, and love in the face of violence. The strength and wisdom we used to press forward still live in us and guide our hearts.

Acknowledge your heritage and embrace the strengths and values it imparts. Resilience in response to specific experiences or situations is described with particular words or statements. Reflect on these connections for self-inquiry or support.

Resilience in Times of Natural Disasters
Studies on resilience during natural disasters can be found across various branches of empirical psychology, focusing on vic-

tims of natural disasters, life-threatening cardiovascular attacks, veterans of extreme hardships such as World War II or the Korean War, former prisoners of war, physical abuse survivors, or war refugees. Many stress-hardy individuals experience remarkable recoveries from severe hardships, indicating that possessing resistance traits can shield individuals from adverse surroundings. Additionally, protective factors and a low number of stress-induced burdens further contribute to safeguarding one's integrity. This section is not a guidebook for patience and modesty but rather an in-depth reflection on adversarial contexts life may present.

- **Tangible and Intangible Support**: Tangible support includes physical help and resources, while intangible support involves emotional and psychological assistance. Both forms of support are crucial in building resilience during and after natural disasters.
- **Core Resources**: Core resources such as a stable home, access to food and water, and community support systems are essential for maintaining resilience in the face of natural disasters.

Resilience in Times of Economic Hardship

Economic conditions have changed dramatically over time. During the Great Depression of the 1930s, mutual cooperation and local rescue programs were essential for survival. Families relied on mental acumen and personal interactions to get through tough times. The phrase "making do" emerged, signifying the ability to get along with what one has and make the best of it. This mindset of resilience, cooperation, and ingenuity can be valuable in today's economic challenges.

- **Community Cooperation**: Cooperation among community members was vital during past economic hardships. People took on odd jobs, exchanged services, and bartered for necessities, relying on each other to get through tough times.
- **Spiritual and Emotional Resilience**: Maintaining one's spirit, countenance, and emotional openness was crucial for survival. Faith and values were transferred in innovative ways, helping individuals and communities cope with economic difficulties.

Learning from Historical Resilience

Reflecting on historical resilience, such as the experiences during the Great Depression, can offer valuable lessons for today's challenges. The resilience, cooperation, and ingenuity of past generations can inspire current and future generations to face adversity with strength and determination.

Chapter 9: The Role of Social Support in Building

The Importance of Social Support

When people lack access to information, resources, and social connections, their ability to address adversity diminishes. This limited capacity increases feelings of stress and prolongs adverse situations. Under intense stress, individuals often withdraw from their families, friends, and colleagues, further reducing personal resources and available support. This withdrawal limits the help they receive and decreases the range of perspectives and information they could access through frequent social interactions. Lack of social support is not confined to the underprivileged; even in resource-rich environments, individuals can experience diminished support if their close relationships lack emotional depth or helping behaviors.

Social support is crucial for building resilience. It provides emotionally sustaining relationships and opportunities to focus on others and the broader environment, moving beyond self-centered concerns. Social support offers diverse perspectives and problem-solving strategies, giving individuals the intellectual and emotional resources needed to address adversity constructively. Increased social connections provide options for feedback on potential actions and alternative viewpoints, boosting self-confidence. Seeking help for personal problems can prevent individuals from feeling burdened, and counselors can encourage self-assessment and reevaluation.

Family Support

Family support, whether from nuclear family members or 'fictive kin' such as close friends, forms a critical core for most people. Being able to depend on family without justifying every need or request is what defines a supportive family. This backing significantly enhances one's ability to function in various aspects of life. However, this should not be confused with stressed family members who rush to rescue their ill family member or friend too quickly. Family support must be balanced with the necessity for all members to have their own lives.

For example, individuals living with multiple sclerosis (MS) often face unique challenges in balancing their needs with family dynamics. While they may appreciate their family's care and understanding, they also strive not to feel like a burden. Effective family support involves understanding these dynamics and providing help in a way that respects everyone's challenges and periods of difficulty.

Peer Support Networks

The positive health and psychological benefits of peer support are well-documented. Peer support has been effective in addressing various problem areas. It aids recovery by showing individuals they are not alone and providing hope that adaptation is possible. Peers serve as models of successful recovery, reinforcing the idea that it is achievable. Societal well-being is vulnerable to rapid or violent changes, which can undermine health. Across cultures, people seek peer support to manage changes. Encouraging communities to systematically use peer support interventions can significantly enhance resilience.

Research shows that our social environment and the people we surround ourselves with matter significantly. Peers can influence the neural mechanisms guiding and controlling our stress response system. Together, we can develop greater awareness of our stress responses and take collective actions to challenge emotions like fear and anger, replacing them with gratitude, compassion, and kindness. Our biological connection to social networks makes it natural to turn to others in times of stress.

Conclusion

Social support is a critical component of resilience. It provides emotional sustenance, diverse perspectives, and problem-solving strategies. Family and peer support networks play essential roles in helping individuals manage adversity and build resilience. By fostering supportive relationships and communities, we can enhance our collective ability to withstand and recover from life's challenges.

{ **10** }

Chapter 10: Resilience and Innovation

The Role of Innovation in Fostering Resilience

Innovation creates the need for adaptation and can significantly enhance resilience. Changing the rules can strengthen already resilient structures by creating new knowledge about our complex world and acting on evidence to guard against surprises or catastrophic failures. However, a key challenge is overcoming the narrow focus on physical, biological, or other quantifiable risk fields to understand innovation as a force for environmental resilience.

"Innovation" refers to the process of translating information into new, more reliable goods, services, or fields of human endeavor. Generations of innovators have driven economic, social, and intellectual progress by identifying and connecting previously unrecognized elements to create value. Successful innovation often occurs in organizations where skills, knowledge, capital, and ideas are combined in focused environments. Despite its challenges and frustrations, innovation is crucial for progress. It is inherently a journey into the unknown and is subject to the same stresses and nonlinear perturbations that drive systems organized by creative destruction.

Resilience and Creativity

For artists and creators, resilience is a critical antidote. They face not only common hurdles and setbacks but also the uncertainties of living without a predictable support system. Human suffering has long inspired the creative arts, with great drama, art, music, and literature portraying tragic characters and heart-rending struggles. According to one survey of Millennial students, a career in the arts is highly valued for its meaning and purpose. The arts play a vital role in Western culture and are often supported to alleviate suffering.

Resilience enables artists to persist despite challenges, using their experiences to fuel their creativity and produce meaningful work. The process of creating art involves navigating uncertainties, finding inspiration in adversity, and drawing strength from personal and collective histories.

Adapting to Technological Changes

The rapid pace of technological change has raised concerns about job polarization and inequality. Automation is likely to impact many jobs, such as drivers, pilots, and office clerical workers, as new opportunities are not always equitably distributed. As tech giants accumulate wealth and hire fewer workers while increasing productivity, income inequality grows. Successful societies in the 21st century will be those with a richer social fabric and wider income distributions, leveraging the human skills of their populations.

Technological changes have disrupted established social norms. Automation and digital technologies continue to accelerate, with many jobs created by the industrial revolution now threatened by artificial intelligence and machine learning. Jobs less susceptible to automation are non-routine and require analysis, creativity, and interpersonal skills. Future employment will depend more on soft skills and emotional intelligence. Education must adapt to help people develop these skills and navigate changing employment dynamics. With longer lifespans, individuals are likely to change careers multiple times, making retraining a norm rather than an exception.

Embracing Innovation and Resilience

Resilience and innovation are intertwined. Adapting to technological changes, leveraging creativity, and fostering supportive environments are essential for building resilience in the face of modern challenges. By embracing innovation and developing skills for the future, individuals and societies can thrive amid uncertainty and change.

{ 11 }

Chapter 11: Resilience in Leadership

The Need for Resilient Leaders

There has been much discussion about the importance of leaders being resilient. Traditional 'command and control' management styles have been largely rejected in favor of approaches that emphasize teamwork, vision-sharing, and effective communication. While the image of a heroic leader who single-handedly brings success can be appealing, many now recognize the drawbacks of relying too heavily on one individual. Instead, modern leadership focuses on building and engaging teams, sharing responsibilities, and fostering a culture of resilience within organizations.

Effective leadership is essential for navigating challenges and achieving success. Outstanding leaders are often judged by their ability to cope creatively and effectively with difficulties while guiding teams or entire organizations. Defining effective leadership provides a benchmark for selection and psychological testing, helping organizations measure and develop leadership qualities. In challenging times, leaders must cultivate their resilience to provide the understanding, support, and encouragement their teams need to thrive.

Leadership Styles that Foster Resilience

Different leadership styles can condition, shape, and direct the attitudes, behaviors, and development of employees and organization members. These leadership processes allow employees to share leadership responsibilities, creating a unified understanding of organizational culture and direction. Resilient leaders consciously choose styles that fulfill social needs and give greater meaning and connectedness to their work, employees, and the broader world.

- **Caregiving Leadership**: Focuses on nurturing and supporting employees, fostering a sense of identification and belonging.
- **Entrepreneurial Leadership**: Encourages innovation and risk-taking, providing employees with the freedom to think and act responsibly.
- **Transformational Leadership**: Inspires and motivates employees to achieve their highest potential by aligning personal and organizational goals.
- **Shared Leadership**: Distributes leadership responsibilities across the team, promoting collaboration and collective decision-making.

Leading Teams Through Adversity

Organizations face rising levels of business turmoil due to factors like global warming, industrial change, and infrastructure failure. These challenges demand agility, innovation, and automation processes to maintain competitive advantage. The impact on team members, led by individuals with increasing workplace pressures, is significant, leading to stress-related problems. Teams rarely revert to their previous status quo after crises;

they either become more cohesive and efficient or more dysfunctional and demoralized.

Poor well-being among team members can demotivate individuals, reduce performance outcomes, and increase psychological costs for organizations. In their book, "The Art of Resilience: Thriving in the Face of Adversity," Carole Pemberton, Rob Worrall, and Judith Kamps explore the value of resilience in the workplace. They offer guidance on becoming more resilient when setbacks seem endless and pressures overwhelming.

The chapter examines the nature and experience of adversity, its impact on team well-being, and the role of team leaders in such demanding times. It draws on organizational psychology to apply the Resilience Framework for creating resilient teams. Effective leadership can strengthen team tolerance to adversity and support overall well-being.

Conclusion

Resilient leaders are essential for guiding teams through adversity and achieving success. By adopting leadership styles that foster resilience, leaders can condition and shape the development of their teams, promoting a culture of collaboration and mutual support. Understanding and applying the principles of resilience can help organizations navigate challenges and thrive in an ever-changing environment.

Chapter 12: Measuring and Assessing Resilience

Measuring Resilience at a Social Level

Initial efforts to measure resilience at a social level are promising, and it's crucial to further develop these measures. Fostering resilience in individuals, families, and communities requires identifying the critical components of resilience at the social level. This approach goes beyond recognizing basic building blocks and processes, aiming to construct actuarial tables that can predict resilience. These tables would be based on salient traits and attributes that interact with environmental dimensions at the individual, family, school, and neighborhood levels. Such measures could accurately forecast resilience in children and youth, allowing for more appropriate allocation of treatment resources.

Conceptualizing and Characterizing Resilience

Conceptualizing resilience is challenging, and characterizing it with specific mechanisms and processes is even more daunting. Significant progress has been made in assessing resilience through neurological structure and function. Studies focus on identifying potential biomarkers that can be measured and assessed. For instance, linking adversity with potential biomarkers enables the assessment of adversity's impact on biochemical, molecular, and neurological functioning. Identifying biomarkers of resilience can stimulate new research mechanisms and targets for intervention.

Resilience Scales and Instruments

Several scales and instruments have been developed to measure resilience, evaluating factors such as personal strengths, sense of control, problem-solving abilities, and coping skills. These tools help researchers gauge the perceived success of individuals and the benefits or lessons learned from adversity. Some key scales include:

- **Resilience Scale**: Measures positive outcomes in clients with symptoms of posttraumatic stress disorder (PTSD). It evaluates personal strengths, sense of control, problem-solving abilities, and coping skills.
- **Trauma Adaptation Scale**: Assesses how individuals adapt to trauma and adversity.
- **Perceived Benefits Scale**: Evaluates the benefits perceived by individuals after experiencing adversity.
- **Perceived Positive Life Changes Scale**: Measures the positive changes individuals perceive in their lives following adversity.
- **Positive Change Scale**: Assesses the degree of positive change individuals experience after adversity.

These scales serve as quick assessment tools for preliminary work before developing more extensive measures. Research with these scales can identify long-term resilience in individuals and institutions.

Evaluating Resilience Programs

Despite calls for evidence-based programming, there has been limited ex post evaluation to determine the effectiveness of resilience interventions. To design and implement effective programs, it's crucial to understand the process that generates resilience. Ex ante evaluations should first consider whether resilience is an appropriate framework for a given context, the timing of interventions, and the beneficiaries of resilience.

Future research should focus on:

- **Clear Understanding of Resilience**: Defining resilience and the processes through which it emerges.
- **Targeting Malleable Aspects**: Designing programs that effectively target aspects of resilience that can be influenced.
- **Methodologies for Identifying Change**: Developing methodologies to identify changes in resilience over time.

Evidence-based programming in resilience is essential for developing effective interventions that promote resilience in various contexts.

{ 13 }

Chapter 13: Ethical Considerations in Resilience R

Ethical Considerations in Mitigating Distress

Resilience research must address basic ethical considerations to mitigate distress and establish a universal set of principles and practices. Researchers should transparently communicate the use of resilience research by institutions and funders, ensuring that it supports social justice. Using diverse experiences and the ethical guidelines of organizations like the National Aboriginal Health Organization, researchers can map ethical issues to various research paradigms and offer guidelines for conducting resilience research. This reflection helps researchers consider the ethical ramifications of their activities, especially when resilience fails.

Informed Consent in Resilience Studies

Respectful data collection is essential when working with survivors of societal trauma. Researchers should anticipate the possibility of participants grappling with painful pasts and approach them with sensitivity. Advances in trauma treatment mean not all participants manage alone or in silence, and their experiences need to be heard and respected. Courtesy calls and initiating personal contacts can help appreciate negative responses or required modifications in participation.

Informed consent is particularly critical when research participants include young children. The presence of researchers can abruptly modify children's daily routines and familiarity anchors, impacting their willingness to share personal accounts. Researchers must address basic voluntariness, privacy, and confidentiality issues and ensure that participants fully understand their involvement in the study.

Protecting Vulnerable Populations

Protecting vulnerable populations is essential, and institutional mechanisms should facilitate access and provide treatment for displaced individuals. Family assistance centers, supported by service-learning environments, are ideal for training future mental health care workers to serve affected populations. The Centers for Disease Control and Prevention (CDC) provides comprehensive materials for planners and service providers related to disaster and specific needs populations. These materials promote emergency preparedness and response for community members with special health care needs.

Natural disasters pose challenges to delivering critical services to vulnerable populations, including children, people with chronic diseases and disabilities, single mothers, and the elderly. Traditional programs often help these individuals, but natural disasters require additional efforts to ensure their safety and well-being. In the United States, a significant portion of households are homeless, and emergency centers often lack resources to serve these populations. Researchers advocate for specific allocations of resources for disaster impact, focusing on the elderly, individuals in nursing homes, people with disabilities and chronic illnesses, and those seeking treatment for mental health conditions and substance abuse.

Guidelines for Ethical Resilience Research

Ethical resilience research should:

- **Mitigate Distress**: Address basic ethical considerations to minimize participant distress.
- **Ensure Transparency**: Communicate the use of resilience research transparently, supporting social justice.
- **Respect Informed Consent**: Obtain informed consent, ensuring participants understand their involvement and addressing privacy and confidentiality.
- **Protect Vulnerable Populations**: Implement mechanisms to support vulnerable populations, particularly during disasters.

By following these guidelines, researchers can conduct resilience studies ethically and responsibly, ensuring the well-being of participants and the integrity of their work.

{ 14 }

Chapter 14: The Future of Resilience Research

Expanding Empirical Support for Resilience Programs
Currently, there is more theoretical writing about fostering resilience than empirical support for existing programs. There is a critical need for experimental trials aimed at fostering protective processes in individuals and communities to address multiple risks. Traditional risk-reduction strategies, such as reducing poverty and providing good prenatal care, often contrast with resilience-specific approaches. A transactional model suggests focusing primary prevention efforts on areas most malleable during development with the greatest impact across multiple outcomes. Individuals and communities disconnected from typical support sources may benefit from targeted interventions fostering protection-specific risk-reduction approaches.

A thorough understanding of resilience through rigorous research techniques is essential for guiding future research and informing intervention and prevention initiatives. Addressing how to foster resilience in different contexts and cultures is a pressing issue. An unfortunate divide currently exists between research understanding the processes influencing the etiology of problems and research fostering protections to disrupt predictive links between adversities and long-term problems. Large-scale, interdisciplinary experimental projects aimed at fostering resilience in real-world conditions are needed to bridge this gap.

Emerging Trends in Resilience Studies

The concept of resilience has been enriched with various dynamics, including biodiversity, regulation fluidity, local knowledge, migration, historical consciousness, learning relationships, and investing in human, relational, and social capital. However, there has been little attention to comparing and evaluating these dynamics. The dynamic discourse on resilience offers lessons for policy and management, reflecting the flexibility of resilience as a concept and resource.

The resilience concept has spread across different disciplines, justifying reforms, promoting new policies, and being considered in various fields. Borrowed from ecology, it has become popular in urban studies and social sciences. In economics and sociology, resilience is linked to facing insecurity and vulnerability, while in management and business administration, it refers to the capacity of large systems to adapt to contextual changes.

Increased awareness of resilience among scholars and the public has led to many approaches, models, theories, and empirical studies focusing on resilience. This chapter presents three emerging trends in resilience studies at multiple levels of analysis:

1. **Resilience in a Dynamic Environment**: Understanding how resilience operates in constantly changing conditions.
2. **Expanding the Visual of the Resilience Process**: Broadening the perspective on resilience processes across different contexts.
3. **Emerging Issues in Resilience Research**: Identifying new challenges and opportunities in resilience research.

Interdisciplinary Approaches to Resilience

Different types of potential collaborations include multidisciplinary, interdisciplinary, and cross-disciplinary studies:

- **Multidisciplinary Studies**: Researchers in different fields work independently on a shared problem without collaboration.
- **Interdisciplinary Studies**: Researchers with different expertise work jointly on a shared problem.
- **Cross-Disciplinary Studies**: Researchers from diverse fields create a new discipline, integrating methods and concepts from multiple fields.

Holistic, cross-disciplinary approaches leverage complementary viewpoints and methods to promote resilient provisioning of services by critical infrastructure systems, such as rail, air, maritime, post, and power.

Interdisciplinary approaches address general systemic resilience across different domains, while cross-disciplinary approaches compare, contrast, and combine specialist disciplines to study domain-dependent resilience characteristics. This chapter reviews studies and research results on general systemic resilience, economic systemic resilience, organizational systemic resilience, ICT service resilience, software service resilience, and system recovery, highlighting existing approaches to answering "what is resilience?" from an interdisciplinary perspective. The recently created epic resolver framework exemplifies a cross-disciplinary approach to infrastructure investing, integrating concepts from infrastructure management, resilience engineering, and iterative and agile software development.

Chapter 15: Conclusion and Practical Applications

The Value of Fostering Resilience

Fostering resilience is not only beneficial in treatment settings but also in educational environments. Many teachers incorporate strategies to foster resilience in their students, particularly those who have experienced significant hardship. Often, teachers are motivated by their resilience processes. There has been a growing push to include resilience-fostering programs in schools, and progress has been made. Schools have long provided activities to help students manage stress, and recent programs are associated with declines in reported stress levels among students.

Understanding resilience has practical applications in clinical settings, workplaces, and larger society. Throughout this course, we have discussed various applications. While questioning common-sense views of resilience, both scientific and caring perspectives highlight its allure. Fostering resilience has meaningful consequences, especially when supported by interrelated protective contexts. Enhancing resilience can improve clients' quality of life, which is of central interest in delivering psychological and medical services. Often, addressing specific problems reflects a symptom-reduction approach to emotional health.

Applying Resilience Strategies in Daily Life

Encouraging strong relationships is fundamental to resilience. Being connected to family, friends, and other caring individuals helps combat potential negative effects of poverty. Investing time and effort in your network of close relationships, and connecting to community outlets such as faith-based organizations and neighborhood centers, strengthens support systems. Large extended families provide strong internal support and connect individuals to additional help and information. Stronger networks promote general health in adults and help children achieve developmental milestones and success in school.

Parents and caregivers can help children learn resilience through daily routines and demands of life. Encouraging certain beliefs and actions, creating a home environment with realistic risks, responsibility, and constructive stressors helps everyone grow. A child in a nurturing environment can also help a parent or caregiver become more resilient. This synergy means a resilient family fosters more resilient individuals. Here are some basic concepts to boost resilience in children:

- **Foster Strong Relationships**: Encourage connections with family and community.
- **Promote Independence**: Allow children to take on age-appropriate responsibilities.
- **Model Resilient Behavior**: Demonstrate how to handle challenges and setbacks positively.

Building Resilient Communities

Resilience to disasters is fundamentally about community actions and reactions. Disaster plans and ensuring disaster response entities can function under overwhelming circumstances are crucial. Practical training exercises, acquiring the latest equipment, and investing in communications networks are important. However, resilience also involves what happens in a community before and after a catastrophe. A thriving community that values sustainable choices will respond and recover better from adversity.

Witnessing human perseverance, despite the devastation of disasters, connects us in a shared understanding of the role of stabilizing communities. Building resilience ensures the human spirit, the strength of hope, and the power to make positive changes. Planners often focus on infrastructure, but true resilience involves addressing the root causes of resilience problems. Infrastructure without connected end nodes becomes a stranded asset.

www.ingramcontent.com/pod-product-compliance
Lightning Source LLC
Chambersburg PA
CBHW030403160726
47992CB00007B/2943